MW00424000

THE
LITTLE LOCAL
VERMONT
COOKBOOK

LITTLE LOCAL
VERMONT
COOKBOOK

Recipes for Classic Dishes

MELISSA PASANEN

THE COUNTRYMAN PRESS
A division of W. W. Norton & Company
Independent Publishers Since 1923

Copyright © 2020 by Connected Dots Media
Illustrations by Courtney Jentzen

All rights reserved
Printed in the United States of America

For information about permission to reproduce selections from this book, write to
Permissions, The Countryman Press, 500 Fifth Avenue, New York, NY 10110

For information about special discounts for bulk purchases, please contact
W. W. Norton Special Sales at specialsales@wwnorton.com or 800-233-4830

Manufacturing by Versa Press
Book design by Debbie Berne
Production manager: Devon Zahn

Library of Congress Cataloging-in-Publication Data

Names: Pasanen, Melissa, author.
Title: The little local Vermont cookbook : recipes for classic dishes / Melissa Pasanen.
Description: First edition. | New York, NY : The Countryman Press, a division of
W. W. Norton & Company Independent Publishers since 1923, [2020] | Series: Little
local cookbooks | Includes index.
Identifiers: LCCN 2020001986 | ISBN 9781682685211 (hardcover) |
ISBN 9781682685228 (epub)
Subjects: LCSH: Cooking—Vermont. | Cooking, American—New England style. |
LCGFT: Cookbooks.
Classification: LCC TX715.2.N48 P3725 2020 | DDC 641.59743—dc23
LC record available at https://lccn.loc.gov/2020001986

The Countryman Press
www.countrymanpress.com

A division of W. W. Norton & Company, Inc.
500 Fifth Avenue, New York, NY 10110
www.wwnorton.com

10 9 8 7 6 5 4 3 2 1

In honor of Enid Wonnacott, a champion of Vermont farmers, who drew community together around good food

CONTENTS

Main Courses

Desserts

INTRODUCTION

Here in Vermont, we like to say, you can eat the landscape.

Bite into a fresh green hillside covered with spring's first fiddleheads or aromatic wild ramps. Chomp into a golden summer field of corn or nibble through rows of jewel-bright strawberries. Crunch into a tart apple as if you're savoring the crisp skyline, blazing with fall foliage. Swallow the sweet puffs of maple steam that rise from sugarhouses tucked into snowy winter woods.

As you drive through the landscape of Vermont, on winding country roads between covered bridges and red barns, you will never be too far from a delicious destination. The Green Mountain State has long been a leader in the locavore movement, and we value the many ways our food, drink, and agricultural traditions contribute to our vibrant communities.

Even though—or, perhaps, because—Vermont is so small, we are a feisty and independent lot who prefer to carve our own path in everything from politics to food. Nature is always close by, and we treasure it.

Vermonters tend to count farmers among their friends. We know where our food comes from.

We have more cheesemakers, craft brewers, and farmers' markets per capita than any other state, and we are the nation's leading producer of maple syrup. Visitors to Vermont can follow not only well-traveled hiking and snow-sport trails, but also a cheese trail, a maple trail, and a brewery trail, among others.

In this little book, we celebrate not only the ingredients and recipes produced by the natural and cultural landscape of Vermont, but also the people and traditions that have shaped our menu.

BREAKFAST AND BRUNCH

GINGER MAPLE PUMPKIN MUFFINS

Makes 12 muffins

Hearty and wholesome, with warm, spicy notes, these muffins smell like fall in Vermont. They are the perfect fuel for a hike up Camel's Hump to enjoy spectacular views of a landscape shimmering with red, orange and gold foliage. Mashed winter squash or sweet potato can substitute beautifully for pumpkin.

1¾ cups white whole wheat or all-purpose flour

1 teaspoon baking powder

1 teaspoon baking soda

¾ teaspoon ground cinnamon

½ teaspoon ground ginger

¾ teaspoon salt

2 large eggs

½ cup canola oil

½ cup maple syrup, preferably dark

½ cup light brown sugar

⅓ cup plain or vanilla yogurt

1 teaspoon pure vanilla extract

1 cup mashed pumpkin

½ cup finely chopped crystallized ginger, optional

1 Heat the oven to 400°F. Line a 12-cup muffin tin with paper liners or generously grease muffin cups.

2 In a medium bowl, whisk together the flour, baking powder, baking soda, cinnamon, ginger, and salt.

3 In a large bowl, whisk the eggs and then whisk in the oil, maple syrup, brown sugar, yogurt, and vanilla extract. Add the pumpkin and whisk until well until blended.

4 Add the flour mixture to the pumpkin mixture and stir with a spoon just until well combined. Stir in the crystallized ginger, if using, and evenly scoop the batter into the prepared muffin cups.

5 Reduce the heat to 375°F and bake until the muffins are golden and a toothpick or cake tester inserted in the center comes out clean, 18 to 20 minutes. Remove from the oven and set aside on a cooling rack at least 10 minutes before eating.

Note: Maple syrup grading used to vary across North America, but the grades are now standardized. Golden is the lightest and most delicate in taste; it's used for pouring over everything from pancakes to ice cream. Amber, with its deeper flavor and color, is good for both drizzling and cooking. Dark, the most robust, is preferred for baking by many Vermont cooks.

VERMONT HONEY AND MAPLE GRANOLA

Makes about 8 cups

Hippies and back-to-the-landers flocked to Vermont during the 1960s and '70s, and they had a major impact on the state's culture, including, perhaps, our fondness for granola. I like mine chunky, so I use local honey along with maple syrup, and I let it cool completely on the baking sheet. Don't skip the salt unless your health prohibits it—it balances the sweetness.

⅓ cup olive or canola oil

⅓ cup dark maple syrup

⅓ cup honey

¾ teaspoon kosher or coarse sea salt

3 cups rolled oats

3 cups raw nuts or seeds, such as almonds, cashews, pecans, pistachios, pumpkin seeds, or sunflower seeds

2 cups dried fruit, such as sweetened, tart cherries; cranberries; golden raisins; or snipped dried apricots

1 Heat the oven to 325°F. Line a large, rimmed baking sheet or shallow roasting pan with a nonstick baking liner or parchment paper.

2 In a small bowl, whisk together the oil, maple syrup, honey, and salt.

3 In a large bowl, mix together the oats and nuts. Pour the wet mixture over the dry mixture and toss with a rubber spatula until everything is evenly coated. Spread the granola mixture evenly in the prepared pan.

4 Bake for 15 minutes and then stir. Return to the oven and bake until golden brown, 10 to 12 minutes. Remove from the oven.

5 Set aside on a cooling rack (do not touch until it is completely cool). Break the granola into desired-size clumps and mix in the dried fruit. Store in an airtight container.

VERY BERRY BAKED FRENCH TOAST

Makes 12 servings

Berries are one of many delicious reasons that visitors flock to Vermont, from the first sun-kissed strawberries of June all the way through blueberry and raspberry season and then finishing up with the wild blackberries of late summer and early fall. Should you find yourself with a hungry houseful, whip up this quick overnight French toast. It works equally well with fresh or frozen berries, takes about 15 minutes to pull together, and is ready to pop in the oven in the morning. The crunchy topping gilds the lily.

FOR THE FRENCH TOAST

Unsalted butter for greasing

6 large eggs

2 cups whole milk

½ cup dark maple syrup

2 teaspoons pure vanilla extract

1 teaspoon ground cinnamon

½ teaspoon salt

20 ounces sturdy white sandwich bread, sliced ½ inch thick and quartered

1 8-ounce package cream cheese, cut into ¼-inch cubes

2 cups fresh or frozen berries (halve any large strawberries)

½ cup light brown sugar, firmly packed

FOR THE TOPPING

1½ cups rolled oats

¾ cup roughly chopped pecans, optional

8 tablespoons (1 stick) unsalted butter, at room temperature

½ cup dark maple syrup, plus more for serving

Fresh berries for serving, optional

Make the French toast:

1 Grease a 9-by-13-inch baking dish with butter.

2 In a large bowl, whisk together the eggs, milk, maple syrup, vanilla, cinnamon, and salt.

3 Pour half the liquid into the prepared baking dish. Arrange half the bread in the liquid, creating a single layer. Scatter the cream cheese cubes evenly over the bread. Top evenly with the berries and brown sugar. Arrange the remaining bread over the top and pour the remaining liquid evenly over the bread. Press down with a spatula.

4 Use butter to grease a piece of foil large enough to cover the dish, and press the foil down onto the French toast. Refrigerate overnight.

5 In the morning, heat the oven to 350°F. Remove the dish from the refrigerator.

6 Bake, covered, for 30 minutes.

Make the topping:

1 In a small bowl, mix together the oats, pecans (if using), butter, and ½ cup maple syrup until combined.

2 After the first 30 minutes of baking, uncover the French toast and add the topping, pressing it in lightly. Return to the oven and bake until the topping is golden and crunchy and the French toast is puffy, about another 30 minutes. Remove from the oven and set aside to cool for at least 10 minutes before serving.

3 Serve with more maple syrup and fresh berries as desired.

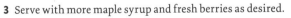

MAPLE BACON SKILLET BISCUITS

Makes 16 biscuits

Vermonters simply cannot eat breakfast without maple syrup in some form. It's all good, but I guarantee that this sweet-salty combination—maple and bacon over tender buttermilk drop biscuits—will become a tradition in your family, as it has in mine. I've lost count of the oohs and ahhs conjured when I flip this caramelized beauty out of my cast-iron skillet.

The recipe is slightly adapted from one by PJ Hamel of King Arthur Flour, the nationally known flour company and baking school headquartered in Norwich, Vermont. Pecan halves are a great substitute for the bacon if desired.

FOR THE TOPPING

Cold unsalted butter for greasing

8 strips bacon, cooked just shy of crisp

¼ cup light brown sugar, firmly packed

2 tablespoons all-purpose flour

3 tablespoons golden or amber maple syrup

2 tablespoons melted unsalted butter

FOR THE BISCUITS

2 cups all-purpose flour

2 teaspoons baking powder

½ teaspoon salt

4 tablespoons (½ stick) very cold unsalted butter, cut into small pieces

1 cup cold buttermilk

Make the topping:

1 Set a rack in the top third of the oven and heat to 475°F. Liberally grease an 8- or 9-inch cast-iron skillet or round cake pan with butter.

2 Chop the bacon into ½-inch pieces. In a small bowl, combine the bacon with the remaining topping ingredients, stirring until well combined. Spread the topping in the bottom of the prepared skillet.

Make the biscuits:

1 In a medium bowl, whisk together the flour, baking powder, and salt. Using your fingers, work in the butter until the mixture has a crumbly texture, retaining some pea-sized pieces of butter. Using a spoon, stir in the buttermilk, forming a sticky dough.

2 Drop the biscuit dough in heaping tablespoonfuls over the topping in the pan, starting with one biscuit in the center and then making two roughly concentric circles around it.

3 Bake for 10 minutes. Turn the oven off and leave the biscuits inside until golden brown and the edges of the center biscuit look fully baked, 5 to 7 minutes.

4 Remove from the oven and immediately lay a serving plate larger than the skillet on top. Carefully flip over. Lift off the skillet and scrape any parts of the topping stuck in the skillet onto the biscuits. Allow to cool slightly and serve.

SMOKEHOUSE FRITTATA

Makes 6 to 8 servings

Frittatas are basically a crustless quiche, and they're simpler to make. This one was inspired by a friend's productive chicken flock. The eggs her hens lay come in a beautiful variety of colored shells, everything from the palest sky blue to a freckled shade of milky coffee.

In the old days, Vermont backyards also often had a small smokehouse to preserve hams and other cured meats. A few of our Cheddar-makers here smoke some of their cheese, with delicious results. (Seek out Cheddar that's really smoked and not made with fake smoke flavor.) If you can't find smoked Cheddar, use regular Cheddar instead.

In Vermont, we do like to "eat more kale," as the T-shirts and bumper stickers say—but you can use spinach or chard, if you prefer. This frittata makes a great quick supper, too, when served with a green salad and some crusty bread.

Unsalted butter for greasing

1 tablespoon olive oil

1 cup diced onion

½ teaspoon kosher salt

Freshly ground black pepper

6 ounces ham, diced

3 large kale leaves, stemmed and sliced into ribbons (yields about 3 packed cups)

8 large eggs

1½ cups shredded smoked Cheddar

1 Heat the oven to 375°F. Liberally grease an 8- or 9-inch cast-iron skillet or ovenproof sauté pan of similar diameter that's at least 2 inches deep with butter.

2 In the skillet over medium heat, warm the olive oil until it shimmers. Add the onion, salt, and a few grinds of the black pepper and cook, stirring occasionally, until softened and golden, 4 to 5 minutes.

3 Add the ham and sauté, stirring occasionally, just until it is lightly browned, 4 to 5 minutes. Add the kale and cook, stirring occasionally, until it is tender, 5 to 6 minutes. If the mixture becomes too dry, add a little water.

4 In a medium bowl, whisk the eggs with a few grinds of the black pepper. Stir in 1 cup of the cheese.

5 Reduce the heat to medium-low and pour the egg mixture evenly over the ham and vegetables in the skillet. Cook, using a spatula to push the egg away from the edges as it sets and tilting the pan so uncooked egg flows into the space, until there is just a little uncooked egg remaining, 6 to 7 minutes.

6 Scatter the remaining ½ cup cheese over the frittata and bake until browned, puffy, and completely set (a knife inserted in the center should come out clean), 5 to 7 minutes. Remove from the oven and set aside to rest about 5 minutes before cutting it into wedges and serving.

DRINKS AND APPETIZERS

SWITCHEL

Makes just over 1 quart

Refreshing and restorative, switchels were originally made for farmworkers. As described by the Vermont cookbook icon Mrs. Appleyard, "When the ringing noise of scythes being sharpened ceases and no figures are seen in the hayfield, it is pretty sure that the mowers are passing the switchel jug from hand to hand."

Make a Vermont Dark and Stormy by shaking together 2 ounces of switchel with 1½ ounces dark rum over ice. Finish with 3 ounces of ginger beer and a lime wedge.

⅓ cup cider vinegar, plus more to taste

¼ cup dark maple syrup, plus more to taste

2 tablespoons blackstrap molasses

¾ teaspoon ground ginger

1 quart cold water

Ginger beer, optional

1 In a medium bowl or wide-mouthed pitcher, whisk together the cider vinegar, maple syrup, molasses, and ginger.

2 In a large pitcher or jug, combine the syrup mixture with the water and stir vigorously. Chill for at least 1 hour.

3 Stir well, as the molasses settles during the chilling process. Taste and adjust as desired with more maple syrup or cider vinegar.

4 Drink as is over ice or combine equal parts switchel and ginger beer.

MULLED HOT CIDER

Makes 8 servings

According to a 1980 manual on cider coauthored by Pulitzer Prize-winning novelist and former longtime Vermonter Annie Proulx, "Mulled cider recipes are as numerous as the apples on a mature tree." And, the authors add, "When the winter wind howls outside and snow heaps up on the sill . . . there are few more comforting and soul-satisfying drinks than New England Butter Rum Cider."

Just add a slug of rum and a pat of butter for those very cold nights.

1 orange

8 whole cloves

2 quarts sweet cider

5 cinnamon sticks, broken

6 whole star anise

A few dashes orange bitters, optional

Garnish: 8 whole cinnamon sticks

1 Wash the orange well and evenly stick the cloves in the skin. Cut the orange into quarters.

2 In a large nonreactive pot over medium heat, combine the cider, orange quarters, cinnamon sticks, and star anise and bring to a simmer. Cover and simmer until the spices have seasoned the cider, 10 to 15 minutes. Remove from the heat.

3 Strain the hot cider into mugs. Add a dash of bitters to each serving, if using, and serve each garnished with a cinnamon stick.

HARD CIDER AND CRANBERRY PUNCH

Makes 8 servings

Apples in Vermont go back to the colonial era, when settlers often planted a few trees on their homesteads. Some varieties were stored in barrels "down cellar." Some were dried or cooked down into applesauce. Others were pressed into sweet cider or pressed and then fermented into hard cider—the common tipple of the time.

The last 20 years have seen a renaissance in small-scale hard cidermaking and a rediscovery of traditional cider apples, as well as a growing number of craft distillers that make apple-based spirits, like brandy.

4 ounces apple brandy

8 ounces unsweetened cranberry juice

4 ounces Cinnamon Syrup (recipe follows)

32 ounces hard cider, well chilled

Large ice ring

Garnish: cinnamon sugar, optional

1 In a large pitcher or punch bowl, stir together the apple brandy, cranberry juice, and Cinnamon Syrup. Refrigerate until well chilled.

2 Add the hard cider and large ice ring to the bowl (larger pieces of ice take longer to melt and don't dilute the punch as quickly).

3 If desired, dip the rims of the punch glasses in water and then in the cinnamon sugar, creating sugared rims. Serve.

CINNAMON SYRUP

Makes about 1¼ cups (10 ounces)

1 cup granulated sugar

1 cup water

5 cinnamon sticks, broken into pieces

1 In a small saucepan over medium heat, combine the sugar and water. Bring to a simmer and cook until the sugar is completely dissolved, 10 to 12 minutes.

2 Reduce the heat to low and add the cinnamon. Cover and simmer 25 minutes. Remove from the heat and set aside to cool completely.

3 Strain out the cinnamon and transfer the syrup to a jar with a tight lid for storage. The syrup will keep almost indefinitely stored in the refrigerator.

SMOKED TROUT SPREAD

Makes about 1 cup

In mid-April, trout season opens and anglers eagerly set out for Vermont's streams and rivers, which are by then rushing with the snow melt that cascades down from the mountains. When the catch is good, some of the trout may end up in a smoker, which adds depth of flavor to the tender, sweet flesh. Serve this spread with vegetables, crackers, crusty bread, or sturdy potato chips.

6 ounces smoked trout, skin and bones removed

¼ cup plain Greek yogurt

¼ cup mayonnaise

2 teaspoons freshly squeezed lemon juice

2 teaspoons snipped fresh chives

1 tablespoon snipped fresh dill

1 teaspoon prepared horseradish, plus more to taste

¼ teaspoon kosher salt, plus more to taste

Garnish: fresh chives or dill

1 In a small bowl, flake the trout apart using a fork. Add the remaining ingredients and mix until well combined. Chill for at least 1 hour.

2 Taste and add more horseradish or salt as desired.

3 Immediately before serving, sprinkle with the chives or dill. Serve.

SPIKED
MAPLE-GLAZED NUTS

Makes 3 cups

These nuts make great gifts when presented in glass jars.

3 cups mixed raw nuts, such as whole almonds or pistachios, or halved pecans or cashews

2 tablespoons unsalted butter

¼ teaspoon ground ginger

¼ teaspoon smoked paprika

¼ teaspoon chili powder

¼ teaspoon kosher salt

½ cup dark maple syrup

1 tablespoon whiskey, optional

1 Heat the oven to 350°F. Line a rimmed baking sheet with a non-stick baking liner or parchment paper.

2 In a large, dry skillet over low heat, toast the nuts while stirring frequently until lightly golden, 6 to 8 minutes.

3 Add the butter, spices, and salt to the skillet and cook, stirring constantly, until the butter melts.

4 Raise the heat to medium and stir in the maple syrup and whiskey, if using. Bring the mixture to a simmer and cook, stirring, until the syrup has thickened, about 5 minutes. Remove from the heat.

5 Scrape the nuts and syrup onto the prepared baking sheet and spread into a single layer. Bake until the nuts are dark golden brown and the syrup coating has hardened, about 10 minutes. Remove from the oven and set aside on a cooling rack until completely set.

6 Break apart and serve.

FORAGER'S FLATBREAD

Makes 12 appetizer servings

Spring is slow to come to Vermont, but you know it's finally arrived when the tightly curled tips of ostrich ferns, known as fiddleheads, emerge tentatively into the warming air. The charmingly shaped greens resemble the scroll at the top of a fiddle—hence the name. Their debut marks the start of the foraging, or wildcrafting, season. It continues with ramps (also called wild leeks) and the first mushrooms, which are then followed by greens, such as nettles and dandelions.

Collecting edible wild plants and fungi calls for a solid knowledge base and responsible harvesting. This Forager's Flatbread can be equally delicious made with cultivated options, such as green garlic, which is the name for young garlic that's thinned by farmers before the bulb is mature. Vermont-made smoked mozzarella cheese adds a campfire woodsiness to this flatbread.

3 tablespoons olive oil

4 to 6 ramps or green garlic, bulbs and leaves thinly sliced

2 teaspoons kosher salt

6 ounces fiddleheads or asparagus tips plus tender stalks (about 1 cup), cut in ½-inch lengths

1 pound mixed foraged or farmed mushrooms, sliced or torn into bite-size pieces

1 pound pizza dough

All-purpose flour for rolling

1½ cups Wild Greens Pesto (recipe follows)

1 8-ounce ball smoked mozzarella, shredded

1 Place a pizza stone or sturdy baking sheet on the center rack of the oven and heat to 450°F.

2 In a large sauté pan over medium heat, warm 1 tablespoon of the oil. Add the ramps and ½ teaspoon salt and cook, stirring occasionally, until ramps soften, about 3 minutes.

3 Add the fiddleheads to the pan, cover, and cook until the fiddleheads are just tender but not mushy, about 5 minutes. Transfer the ramp mixture to a bowl and set aside.

4 Add the remaining 2 tablespoons of the oil to the pan and return to medium-high heat. When the oil shimmers, add the mushrooms and the remaining 1½ teaspoons salt. Cook, stirring occasionally, until the mushrooms have given up their liquid, have turned golden, and make a squeaking noise against the pan, 10 to 12 minutes. Remove from the heat.

5 Divide the pizza dough in half. On two well-floured pieces of parchment paper or nonstick baking liners, roll out both halves into rough circles about ½-inch thick.

6 Spread each dough circle with half the Wild Greens Pesto and then scatter half the ramp mixture and half the mushrooms over each. Top each with half the mozzarella.

7 Use the parchment paper or baking liner to carefully transfer one of the flatbreads to the preheated baking stone or baking sheet. Bake until the crust is golden brown and the cheese is bubbling, 10 to 12 minutes. Remove from the oven and repeat with the second flatbread.

8 Serve hot or at room temperature.

Note: Fresh mozzarella is easier to shred if you pop it in the freezer for about 30 minutes before shredding.

· · ·

WILD GREENS PESTO

Makes scant ¾ cup

You can use this "pesto" in many ways that are similar to how you would use traditional basil pesto: tossed with pasta, slathered on grilled bread, or stirred into soft, fresh goat cheese or plain yogurt for a spread or dip.

4 cups greens (wild nettles or dandelion greens; cultivated sorrel; arugula; or tender radish greens), tightly packed

1 ramp or 2 garlic cloves, chopped

3 tablespoons raw nuts or seeds, such as blanched almonds or sunflower seeds

1 tablespoon freshly squeezed lemon juice, plus more to taste

¼ teaspoon kosher salt, plus more to taste

⅓ cup olive oil, plus more to taste

1 In the bowl of a food processor or the jar of blender, combine all ingredients except the olive oil. Blend until smooth, scraping down the sides of the processor as needed.

2 With the machine running, slowly add the olive oil through the feed tube in a steady stream to emulsify. Taste and adjust the levels of the lemon juice, salt, and olive oil as needed to balance the bitterness or tartness of various greens.

Note: Many experts recommend that nettles should be blanched before eating, but I find that when unblanched leaves are finely minced (as they are in this recipe by the food processor), they also lose their sting. If you're concerned, feel free to blanch them first. Squeeze them as dry as possible before proceeding with the recipe.

SOUPS, SALADS, AND SIDES

CHEDDAR ALE SOUP

Makes 6 servings

Cheddar originated in Somerset County in England, and knowledge of how to make it came with early immigrants to New England. The verb "to cheddar" refers to forming cheese curds into slabs, stacking them, and then cutting them.

Vermont is known for its award-winning Cheddars, which are always a natural, pale buttery yellow—never orange, like those from some other states. They range from mild, creamy young Cheddars to bandage-wrapped, multiyear aged Cheddars, which deliver deep, nutty flavor that's often shot through with crystals that melt on the tongue.

This rich soup pairs Vermont's most famous cheese with craft beer, a more recent claim to fame for the state.

4 tablespoons (½ stick) unsalted butter

1 large onion, finely chopped

1 large carrot, scrubbed and finely chopped

1 teaspoon kosher salt, plus more to taste

2 teaspoons minced garlic (about 2 cloves)

1 12-ounce bottle brown or red ale

1 quart chicken or vegetable stock

1 large (10- to 12-ounce) potato, peeled and cut into ½-inch cubes

1 teaspoon minced fresh thyme leaves

1 cup heavy cream

12 ounces sharp Cheddar, grated

Hot pepper sauce, such as Tabasco

Garnish: whole fresh thyme leaves

1 In a large stockpot or Dutch oven, melt the butter over medium-high heat. Add the onion, carrot, and salt and cook, stirring occasionally, until the onions have softened, 5 to 6 minutes. Add the garlic and cook, stirring constantly, 1 minute.

2 Add the ale and bring to a boil. Use a spatula to deglaze the pan, stirring to scrape up any brown bits.

3 Reduce the heat to low and simmer until the volume is reduced by half, 7 to 9 minutes. Add the stock, potato, and minced thyme.

4 Raise the heat to high and bring to a boil.

5 Reduce the heat to medium-low, cover, and simmer until the carrots and potato are completely soft, 10 to 15 minutes. Remove from the heat.

6 Using a stick blender, food processor, or blender, puree the soup until completely smooth. (Be careful when blending hot liquids. Leave the center of the blender lid off or the feed tube of the food processor open, and cover the opening with a wadded-up kitchen towel. Be sure you never overfill your machine.)

7 Return the soup to the pot, if needed, and set over low heat. Stir in the cream and then the Cheddar in handfuls until the cheese is fully incorporated and the soup is smooth and heated to your liking. (Do not allow the soup to boil after adding the cream and cheese, or it may curdle.) Remove from the heat.

8 Add a few drops of hot pepper sauce, taste, and adjust the seasoning as desired. Serve garnished with the whole thyme leaves.

GREEN SALAD
with Cider Honey Vinaigrette

Makes 4 servings

In May, a froth of white and pink blossoms erupts in orchards around Vermont. They're mostly apple trees, but these days, you'll also find local cherries, sour or sweet, and other stone fruit trees. Back in colonial times, wild bees performed the vital task of pollination, but environmental challenges have endangered those populations.

Today, many orchardists engage local beekeepers to bring in their multicolored, stacked hives to ensure a good fruit harvest. This simple salad serves as a sweet-tart reminder that apples need bees of all kinds, as do many other crops.

FOR THE VINAIGRETTE

½ cup sweet cider or natural apple juice

2 tablespoons apple cider vinegar

1 teaspoon honey

1 teaspoon Dijon mustard

½ teaspoon kosher salt, plus more to taste

¼ cup olive oil

FOR THE SALAD

1 small head butter lettuce, leaves torn into bite-size pieces

8 small radishes, thinly shaved

4 to 6 ounces Vermont feta, crumbled

Make the vinaigrette:

1 In a small bowl, whisk together the first five ingredients. While continuing to whisk, gradually add the olive oil in a steady stream. (Alternatively, you can place all the ingredients in a small jar with a tight-fitting lid and shake vigorously until well combined.)

2 Place a little bit of the dressing on a lettuce leaf, taste, and adjust the seasoning as desired.

Make the salad:

In a medium serving bowl, combine the lettuce and radishes. Sprinkle with the feta, dress with the vinaigrette, and serve.

CRUNCHY BROCCOLI SALAD

Makes 8 servings

Home cooks favor different nuts and dried fruits in this community cookbook staple. Some even toss in a cup of shredded Cheddar. Rest the salad a few hours in the refrigerator before serving.

1 scant cup mayonnaise

3 tablespoons honey

3 tablespoons cider vinegar

½ teaspoon kosher salt

Freshly ground black pepper

1½ pounds fresh broccoli crowns, some stems attached

10 strips bacon (about 10 ounces), cooked crisp and crumbled

½ cup roughly chopped pecans, toasted

½ cup golden raisins

½ cup minced red onion

1 In a large serving bowl, whisk together the mayonnaise, honey, cider vinegar, salt, and a few generous grinds of the black pepper.

2 Cut the broccoli florets and peeled stems into bite-size pieces (yields 6 to 7 cups).

3 Set aside some of the bacon and pecans for garnish. Add the broccoli, the rest of the bacon and pecans, the raisins, and onion to the bowl with the dressing. Toss well to combine. Refrigerate for at least 2 hours.

4 Garnish with the reserved bacon and pecans immediately before serving.

ABENAKI THREE SISTERS SALAD

Makes 6 servings

A traditional Native American "three sisters garden" contains corn, squash, and beans, which support each other while also providing a nutritious diet. The Abenaki people were among Vermont's first human inhabitants. Experts now tell us that their gardens probably included two types of squash, sunflowers, Jerusalem artichokes, and ground cherries, too. If you can find them, you can add ground cherries, also called cape gooseberries, to this salad.

½ cup plain Greek yogurt

½ cup buttermilk (preferably not nonfat)

¼ cup minced scallions (including green tops)

1 teaspoon kosher salt, plus more to taste

2 cups fresh corn kernels (about 3 ears)

1½ cups cooked heirloom beans, such as Jacob's Cattle or Marfax, or 1 15-ounce can kidney beans, drained and rinsed

1 medium (12-ounce) zucchini or yellow summer squash, halved lengthwise and thinly sliced into half moons

1 In a medium serving bowl, whisk together the yogurt, buttermilk, scallions, and salt until well blended.

2 Add the corn, beans, and squash to the bowl and toss with the dressing until well coated. Taste and add salt if desired before serving. Serve immediately or chill for 1 hour if desired.

MAPLE MUSTARD ROASTED ROOTS

Makes 8 servings

As long, cold winters dragged into frosty springs, Vermonters depended on cellars full of storage crops like potatoes, parsnips, carrots, beets, and turnips. Parsnips were sometimes left in the ground all winter and then dug up after the ground thawed—the cold turned their starches into sugars, and spring-dug parsnips are still prized for their sweetness.

The state's official vegetable is the Gilfeather turnip, which has even earned a berth in Slow Food USA's Ark of Taste for outstanding flavor and historic merit. Some have dared to suggest that the unusually sweet turnip is actually its milder cousin, the rutabaga, or that perhaps John Gilfeather, who farmed in the southern Vermont town of Wardsboro in the late 1800s, crossed a turnip with a rutabaga. Either way, Wardsboro's annual Gilfeather Turnip Festival, held every October, draws hundreds with a full turnip menu, from turnip doughnuts to scalloped turnips.

Roasted roots make a great side for a holiday ham, and any leftovers can be deployed in a breakfast or brunch hash. Simply dice them up finely and fry them with a little bacon; they make a savory bed for poached or fried eggs.

3 tablespoons olive oil

3 tablespoons amber or dark maple syrup

2 tablespoons whole-grain mustard

1½ teaspoons kosher salt

3 pounds assorted root vegetables, peeled and cut into 1-inch cubes

1 Heat the oven to 425° F.

2 In a small bowl, whisk together the oil, maple syrup, mustard, and salt. Scatter the root vegetables on a rimmed baking sheet and drizzle evenly with the oil mixture.

3 Roast, stirring once or twice, until a fork easily pierces a piece of each vegetable, about 40 minutes. (Some vegetables may be softer than others.) Remove from the oven and serve hot.

MAPLE BAKED BEANS

Makes 6 to 8 servings

The state of Vermont is the largest US producer of maple syrup. Since its founding in 1893, the Vermont Maple Sugar Makers' Association has seen a lot of changes in sugaring technology. Legend tells of a Native American hunter who once notched his hatchet in a sugar maple for safekeeping and then found that a steady drip of lightly sweet sap had fallen into a pot left below. A venison stew that was later cooked in the pot concentrated the sap into a sweet sauce, alerting humans to the value of boiled maple sap.

Some still sugar the old-fashioned way, collecting sap in buckets and boiling it down to syrup in small sugarhouses. This recipe is adapted from one by Mary Gates, who grew up on Howmars Farm in the northern Vermont town of Franklin. She recalls helping with sugaring in the mid-1940s, when she was about 10 years old. The family uses buckets to collect sap to this day, but a tractor has replaced the horses they used back then.

1 pound dry beans, such as yellow eye or Jacob's Cattle

¼ cup plain or maple yogurt, optional (Mary says it helps make the beans more digestible)

1 cup dark maple syrup

1 teaspoon kosher salt, plus more to taste

1 teaspoon dry mustard

5 strips bacon or 4 ounces salt pork, thinly sliced

1 Rinse the beans and pick out and discard any small stones or twigs. Place the beans in a large bowl with the yogurt, if using, and enough water to cover. Stir to combine and soak overnight.

2 Drain the beans and place them in a large, heavy-bottomed, and ovenproof cooking pot with water to cover. Set the pot over high heat and bring to a boil. Remove from the heat, cover, and let the beans sit in the water 30 minutes.

3 Drain again and rinse well. Cover with fresh water and simmer, partially covered, just until you can blow on a bean and the skin cracks—this can take as little as 30 minutes or as long as 2 hours, depending on the type and age of the beans.

4 Heat the oven to 325°F. Drain the beans, reserving their cooking liquid.

5 In a small bowl, whisk together the syrup, salt, and dry mustard. Stir the mixture into the beans. Add some of the cooking liquid, just enough to cover the beans. Lay the bacon over the beans.

6 Bake, covered, for at least 2 hours and up to 5 hours, again depending on the type and age of the beans and also how you like them. Check periodically and add more of the reserved cooking water if the beans become dry. Remove the cover for the last hour to allow the bacon to crisp up. Remove from the oven and serve hot.

MAIN COURSES

BAKED MACARONI AND CHEESE

Makes 6 to 8 servings

There was a time when every Vermont general store had a big wheel of "store cheese" from which wedges of Cheddar were cut to order. Many towns still have a general store where locals head for morning coffee around the wood stove, just to catch up or to spread word of a lost dog. Some sell hot lunches, like homemade macaroni and cheese.

Everyone has a favorite mac and cheese recipe. This version of the quintessential comfort food has a crusty, cheesy top layer and gets a kick from a few dashes of hot sauce.

1 pound elbow macaroni	3 cups milk
4 slices firm white or whole wheat bread	¾ teaspoon kosher salt, plus more to taste
6 tablespoons unsalted butter, plus more for greasing	½ teaspoon freshly ground black pepper
4 packed cups shredded sharp Cheddar (about 1 pound)	Several dashes hot sauce, such as Tabasco
⅓ cup all-purpose flour	

1 Heat the oven to 350°F. Grease a 13-by-9-inch baking dish with the butter.

2 Bring a large pot of heavily salted water over high heat to a boil and stir in the macaroni. Return the pot to a boil and cook, according to package directions, until the macaroni is just cooked but still slightly firm. Remove from the heat. Immediately transfer to a colander to drain and rinse under cold water. Set aside.

3 In a food processor, pulse the bread into chunky crumbs.

4 In a medium saucepan, melt 2 tablespoons of the butter.

5 In a small bowl, mix the breadcrumbs with the melted butter and ½ cup of the cheese. Set aside.

6 Return the saucepan to medium heat and add the remaining 4 tablespoons of butter. When the butter is melted and just starting to foam, whisk in the flour until smooth. Cook, whisking constantly, until golden, about 1 minute. Gradually whisk in the milk and cook, whisking constantly, until a line drawn by your finger across a coated spoon leaves a mark, about 8 minutes. Remove from the heat.

7 Whisk in the salt, black pepper, hot sauce, and the remaining 3½ cups cheese. Taste and add salt or hot sauce as desired.

8 Transfer the macaroni to the prepared baking dish and pour the sauce over it. Mix until well combined. Top evenly with the bread-crumb mixture.

9 Bake until the topping is golden and the sauce is bubbling, 25 to 30 minutes. Remove from the oven and set aside to cool for 10 minutes before serving.

GRILLED TROUT

with Watercress Butter

Makes 4 servings

Peppery wild watercress and shimmering brook trout make
a natural pairing; each can be found in fresh, cold-running
streams during spring in Vermont. There's nothing quite like
the thrill of finding your own food in nature (just make sure
you do so with knowledge and a fishing license!), but you can
also gather farm-raised versions of both in your local grocery
store. Look for small butterflied trout. Purchase them gutted
and boned, without the head, and with the two fillets still
attached along the back.

1½ tablespoons olive oil

4 whole butterflied brook or
rainbow trout (6 to 9 ounces each)

2 teaspoons kosher salt

Freshly ground black pepper

2 cups watercress, coarsely chopped

8 tablespoons (1 stick) unsalted
butter, at room temperature

2 tablespoons minced ramps or
scallions, white and green parts

1 teaspoon freshly
grated lemon zest

Garnish: fresh watercress
sprigs and lemon slices

1 Heat a grill to medium-high. Cut two pieces of foil about 12 by 18 inches and drizzle half the olive oil in the center of each. Pat dry the skin of each trout and season the outside of each with ¼ teaspoon of the salt and generous grinds of the black pepper.

2 Open each trout like a book, flesh side up. Place two on each piece of foil.

3 In a medium bowl, mash together the watercress, butter, ramps, lemon zest, the remaining 1 teaspoon salt, and a few more grinds of the black pepper. Divide the butter mixture roughly in fourths and, using your hands, shape each portion into a small log. Place one log in the center of each open trout and fold each trout closed.

4 Bring the sides of each foil packet together in the center around the two trout, lying side by side. Fold the foil over and seal each packet well.

5 Grill the trout in packets, turning once, about 5 minutes per side. The fish is done when it flakes easily with a fork. Remove from grill.

6 Serve on a bed of fresh watercress with the lemon slices.

CUMIN YOGURT LAMB KEBABS

with Two Sauces

Makes 4 servings

Vermont's pastures were not always sprinkled with dairy cows. In the mid-1800s, the state was all about sheep. Their wool—and waves of immigrants—fueled textile mills. Mill workers from Syria, Lebanon, and Armenia brought their traditional recipes, which often featured lamb. Serve these kebabs with grilled summer vegetables over rice.

1½ cups plain yogurt

1 tablespoon minced garlic (about 3 cloves)

1 tablespoon ground cumin

2 teaspoons kosher salt, plus more to taste

1½ pounds lamb shoulder or leg, cut into 1-inch cubes

2 teaspoons freshly squeezed lemon juice

Emerald Herb Sauce for serving (recipe follows)

1 In a medium bowl, whisk together the yogurt, garlic, cumin, and salt. Transfer ½ cup of the yogurt mixture to a medium container or large zip-top plastic bag. Add the lamb to the container and combine until well coated. Refrigerate 2 to 4 hours.

2 Stir the lemon juice into the remaining cup of yogurt-cumin sauce. Taste and add salt as desired. Refrigerate until ready to use.

3 When ready to cook, heat a grill to medium. Thread the meat onto skewers, making sure not to pack them too tightly.

4 Grill the skewers, turning several times, until evenly browned and cooked through, 10 to 12 minutes. Remove from the grill.

5 Serve with the reserved yogurt-cumin sauce and Emerald Herb Sauce.

. . .

EMERALD HERB SAUCE

Makes about ¾ cup

This bright emerald green sauce makes great use of abundant summer herbs. Lavish it over grilled meats, fish, vegetables, or tofu, or swirl it into yogurt for dipping raw veggies or crusty bread. If you're looking to dress a grain salad, just whisk in more oil and lemon juice.

2 packed cups roughly chopped leaves and tender stems of soft green herbs, such as parsley, basil, oregano, and cilantro	1 tablespoon capers, drained and rinsed
1 tablespoon minced garlic (about 3 cloves)	1 tablespoon freshly squeezed lemon juice plus more to taste
	¼ teaspoon kosher salt, plus more to taste
	⅓ cup olive oil

1 In a food processor, combine the herbs, garlic, capers, lemon juice, and salt and pulse into a paste, scraping down the sides a couple times.

2 While the processor is running, slowly pour the olive oil through the feed tube in a steady stream until the sauce is emulsified. Taste and adjust the levels of salt and lemon juice as desired.

CHICKEN POTPIE

Makes 8 servings

Chicken potpie means something special in Vermont. Instead
of a pastry crust, we cover the savory mixture of chicken,
gravy, and vegetables with a quilt of pillowy biscuits. The dish
is celebrated every fall at chicken pie suppers; some of these
annual events at churches and community centers have been
going strong for close to a century, and multiple seatings sell
out every year.

The secret to light and flaky biscuits is to keep the ingredients cold and work the dough as little as possible. Substitute
turkey for the chicken to make great use of Thanksgiving
leftovers.

FOR THE BISCUITS

3 cups all-purpose flour

2 tablespoons baking powder

1 teaspoon salt

½ teaspoon baking soda

6 tablespoons cold unsalted
butter, cut into small bits

1¼ cups cold buttermilk, plus
a little more for brushing

FOR THE FILLING

6 cups diced cooked chicken

3 cups chicken gravy

1 10-ounce bag frozen peas, thawed

Make the biscuits:

1 Heat the oven to 425°F.

2 In a large bowl, whisk together the flour, baking powder, salt, and
baking soda. Using a pastry blender or fork, work the butter into

the dry ingredients until the mixture is crumbly and still has some pea-sized pieces of butter. Using a wooden spoon, stir in 1¼ cups buttermilk to form a shaggy dough.

3 Lightly flour the counter and dump the dough onto it. Knead it a few times to bring it together and then use a lightly floured rolling pin to roll the dough out to ¾ inch thick. Using a 2½-inch biscuit cutter or a glass, cut out the biscuits. You can reroll scraps only once, as more will make the biscuits tough.

Make the filling:

1 In a large saucepan set over medium heat, stir together the chicken, gravy, and peas. Warm through, stirring occasionally, until bubbling, about 10 minutes. Transfer to a 13-by-9-inch baking dish, making sure the chicken is covered with the gravy (stir in a little water if needed).

2 Arrange the biscuits across the hot filling in rows, about ½ inch apart. Place any extra biscuits on a baking sheet. Brush the biscuits with a little buttermilk.

3 Bake the potpie and extra biscuits until biscuits are golden and filling is bubbling, 15 to 20 minutes. Remove from the oven and serve immediately.

PORK TENDERLOIN

with Cider Thyme Sauce

Makes 4 servings

Pigs have always played an important role in self-sufficient Vermont homesteads, including eating kitchen and farm scraps and providing meat for curing and smoking in backyard smokehouses.

Pork pairs beautifully with all things apple, including this tart-sweet sauce that's made with reduced fresh cider (add a little finely diced apple if you like). Be sure to avoid pork that is preinjected with saline solution, which is sometimes called enhanced pork; the ingredients label should not include salt. Use a sharp knife to remove the thin, shiny sheath of silverskin from the pork before you cook it.

1½ pounds pork tenderloin, silverskin removed

¾ teaspoon kosher salt, plus more to taste

Freshly ground black pepper

1 tablespoon olive oil

1 cup sweet apple cider or natural apple juice

½ cup chicken stock

2 tablespoons unsalted butter

1 tablespoon Dijon mustard

1 tablespoon minced fresh thyme leaves

Garnish: fresh thyme sprigs

1 Heat the oven to 400°F. Rub the pork tenderloin with the salt and several grinds of the black pepper.

2 In a large ovenproof skillet over medium-high heat, warm the oil. Add the pork and cook, turning occasionally, until evenly browned, 7 to 9 minutes.

3 Transfer the skillet to the oven and roast until a thermometer inserted into the thickest part of the pork reads 150 to 160°F (depending how you like your pork cooked), 10 to 12 minutes. Remove from the oven.

4 Remove the pork to a cutting board and tent with foil while you make the sauce.

5 Place the empty skillet over high heat. (Be careful, because the handle will be hot from the oven!) Add the cider and chicken stock and boil, scraping up any brown bits from the bottom of the skillet, 5 to 7 minutes, or until the volume reduces to 1 cup.

6 Reduce the heat to a simmer and whisk in the butter and mustard. Cook, whisking constantly, until the sauce is smooth and glossy, about 1 minute. Stir in the thyme leaves. Taste and add salt or black pepper as desired. Remove from the heat.

7 Serve the sliced pork tenderloin drizzled with the sauce and garnished with the thyme sprigs.

HARVEST STUFFED SQUASH

Makes 6 servings

Fall brings a cornucopia of squash to farm stands and markets: round, ribbed acorn squash; squat pie pumpkins; and the long, striped delicata—my favorite because of its edible skin and quick cooking time. This season of plenty also means you'll find nice fat leeks at the market, and the woods will be filled with mushrooms. On top of that, it's also apple-picking and wild turkey season!

For a vegetarian version, substitute 2½ cups of cooked brown rice and some toasted almonds for the turkey.

3 medium whole winter squash

3 tablespoons olive oil

8 ounces farmed or foraged mushrooms

1½ teaspoons kosher salt

Freshly ground black pepper

1 large carrot, peeled and finely diced

1 large leek, white and light green parts only, chopped and washed well

1 pound ground turkey

1 large apple, cored and diced (no need to peel)

1½ tablespoons minced garlic (about 5 cloves)

1 teaspoon smoked paprika, optional

½ cup grated hard cheese (about 2 ounces), such as cave-aged Orb Weaver or Tarentaise from Thistle Hill Farm or Spring Brook Farm

1 Heat the oven to 400°F.

2 Cut each squash in half across the middle and remove the seeds and stringy bits. Cut a small slice off the stem and the blossom ends of pumpkins or acorn squash so the halves can sit flat on their bottoms.

3 Lightly oil a large rimmed baking sheet with 1 tablespoon of the oil and place the squash on it, flesh side down. Roast until tender and cooked all the way through but not collapsed, 25 to 40 minutes. (This can vary widely depending on variety and size of squash.) Remove from the oven and set aside on the baking sheet, but leave the oven on.

4 Slice or tear the mushrooms into bite-size pieces and toss them in a baking dish with 1 tablespoon of the oil, ½ teaspoon of the salt, and a few grinds of the black pepper. Roast at the same time as the squash until golden and a little crisp at the edges, 15 to 25 minutes depending on the mushroom variety (button mushrooms will take the longest).

5 While the squash and mushrooms are roasting, warm the remaining 1 tablespoon of oil in a large, heavy-bottomed pot over medium heat until it shimmers. Add the carrot and leek and cook, stirring occasionally, until the leek has softened and turns golden, 6 to 8 minutes.

6 Add the turkey, apple, garlic, the remaining 1 teaspoon of salt, and the smoked paprika if using. Mix well and cook, stirring occasionally to break up the meat, until the turkey is cooked through, 8 to 10 minutes. Remove from the heat and stir in the mushrooms. Taste and adjust seasoning as desired.

7 Turn the roasted squash halves onto their bottoms on the rimmed baking sheet. Fill each half generously with the turkey mixture and top each with a sprinkle of the cheese. Return to the oven to melt the cheese and warm through, about 10 minutes. Remove from the oven and serve immediately.

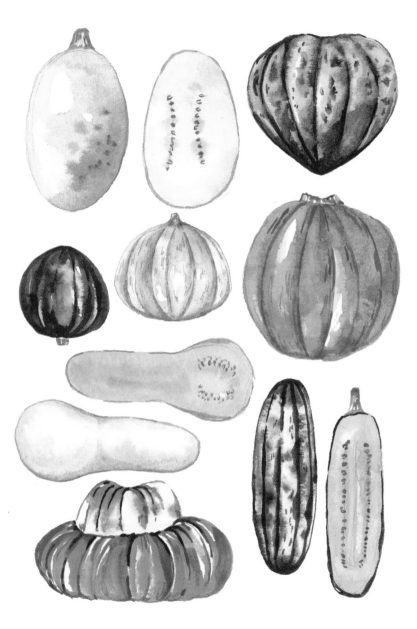

VENISON CHILI

Makes 6 servings

Deer-hunting season is still a big deal in Vermont, both as a cultural tradition and as a way to manage the deer population while providing food. Weekends spent in rustic cabins known as "deer camp" smell of woodsmoke, venison chili, and damp wool shirts.

Ground beef, buffalo, or even turkey work well in place of the venison in this recipe. For a hearty meatless version, use diced butternut squash.

2 tablespoons vegetable oil

1 large onion, diced

2 bell peppers (any color), diced

1 generous tablespoon minced garlic (about 4 cloves)

1 tablespoon chili powder (preferably a smoky one, like chipotle or ancho), plus more to taste

1 tablespoon ground cumin

2 teaspoons kosher salt, plus more to taste

1 pound ground venison

2 tablespoons all-purpose flour

1 28-ounce can diced tomatoes

2 15-ounce cans black beans or kidney beans, drained and rinsed

1 tablespoon cider vinegar

Garnish: chopped fresh cilantro and shredded Cheddar

1 In a large, heavy-bottomed soup pot set over medium-high heat, warm the oil. Add the onion, bell peppers, garlic, chili powder, cumin, and 1 teaspoon of the salt. Sauté until the onion and peppers soften, stirring occasionally, 6 to 8 minutes.

2 Add the venison with the remaining 1 teaspoon of salt and cook, stirring occasionally to break up the meat, until browned, 7 to 10 minutes.

3 Sprinkle in the flour and cook, stirring constantly, for another 2 minutes. Stir in the tomatoes. Raise the heat to high to bring to a simmer.

4 Stir in the beans and lower the heat to maintain the simmer. Cook uncovered, stirring occasionally to prevent sticking, until the chili has thickened, about 20 minutes.

5 Stir in the cider vinegar. Taste and add more chili powder or salt as desired. Cook another 5 minutes. Remove from the heat.

6 Serve garnished with the cilantro and cheese.

DESSERTS

STRAWBERRY RHUBARB CRISP

Makes 8 servings

Fruit crisp has to be among the easiest, most delicious, and versatile desserts around. Here, I combine the first two fruits that pop up in Vermont each spring, but this recipe will work with any New England–grown fruit. In deep summer, try raspberries or tart cherries with sliced peaches; in fall, opt for diced apple and blackberries. If you're using any fruit other than rhubarb or sour cherries, ½ to ¾ cup sugar should be enough to sweeten the filling.

No matter which fruit you use, serving this with vanilla ice cream on top is nonnegotiable.

12 tablespoons (1½ sticks) unsalted butter, at room temperature, plus more for greasing

4 cups hulled and halved strawberries (about 3 pints)

4 cups sliced rhubarb (about 1 pound)

1½ cups granulated sugar

1¼ cups all-purpose flour

2 cups rolled oats

1 cup light brown sugar

1 teaspoon ground cinnamon

½ cup chopped walnuts or pecans, optional

Vanilla ice cream for serving

1 Heat the oven to 350°F. Grease a 13-by-9-inch baking dish with butter.

2 In a large bowl, toss together the strawberries, rhubarb, granulated sugar, and ¼ cup of the flour. Evenly spread the fruit mixture in the prepared baking dish.

3 In the same bowl, stir together the remaining 1 cup flour, oats, brown sugar, and cinnamon. Add the chopped nuts if using. Using your hands, smush the butter into the mixture and squeeze it together until it clumps. Evenly spread the clumps over the fruit, pressing down lightly.

4 Place the baking dish on a rimmed baking sheet to catch any juicy spills and bake until the topping is golden brown and the fruit juices bubble, about 45 minutes. Remove from the oven and set aside to cool about 5 minutes before serving.

5 Serve warm with the ice cream.

MAPLE CREAM PIE

Makes 10 to 12 servings

The very name of our state—which came from *Les Monts Verts*, or the Green Mountains—speaks to the region's historical French connections. French-speaking Quebec is less than 45 miles north of Burlington, and many Vermonters have French Canadian heritage. Among the things we share with our northern neighbors are a love of maple syrup and recipes for maple pie, a smooth, creamy, very sweet, and very rich treat.

Each family swears by its own recipe. Some are made with eggs and some with nuts; some use flour and others, cornstarch. This version is based on one from the late Edith Foulds, a lifelong Vermonter and a champion of the state's maple industry. The black pepper is not optional; you won't exactly taste it, but it adds something special.

If you prefer to go out for your pie, excellent versions can be sampled at The Creamery Restaurant in Danville and the P&H Truck Stop in Wells River.

1½ cups heavy cream

⅓ cup all-purpose flour

1½ cups dark maple syrup

¼ teaspoon fine black pepper
(not freshly ground)

Pinch salt

2 tablespoons unsalted butter

1 9-inch unbaked pie crust

Unsweetened whipped
cream for serving

1 Set a rack in the center position of the oven and heat to 375°F.

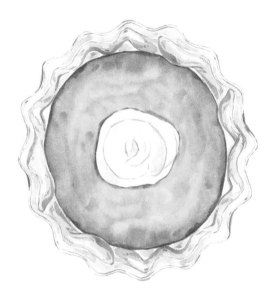

2 In a heavy saucepan, whisk together the cream and flour until smooth. Whisk in the maple syrup, black pepper, and salt. Add the butter. Set the saucepan over medium heat and bring to a simmer. Cook, stirring constantly, until the mixture is the texture of thick custard and thick enough so that a line drawn by your finger across a coated spoon leaves a mark, about 15 minutes. (Do not allow the mixture to boil.)

3 Fit the crust into a pie pan and crimp the edge decoratively. Set the pie pan on a rimmed baking sheet and pour the hot filling into the crust.

4 Bake until the crust is golden and the filling is bubbling evenly, 20 to 25 minutes. Remove from the oven and set aside on a cooling rack until cooled to room temperature.

5 Refrigerate for at least 2 hours to set. Serve with unsweetened whipped cream.

APPLE AND CHEDDAR HAND PIES

Makes 8 hand pies

We joke in Vermont that we love our pie so much, we even eat it for breakfast. Another local tradition is to pair a slice of apple pie with a slice of Cheddar, balancing the sweet with a little savory. As the saying goes: "Apple pie without the cheese is like a hug without the squeeze."

Instead of a standard apple pie, this recipe combines apple and Cheddar to make individual handheld pies (a.k.a. turnovers). You could leave out the Cheddar and increase the amount of apple if you prefer, but give this a try first.

I like to use all-butter puff pastry. Feel free to use other brands, but the size of the package and pastry sheets varies, so adjust accordingly. Choose a tart, firm apple variety or be prepared for applesauce pie, which is not actually a terrible thing.

1 14-ounce package frozen puff pastry, thawed according to package directions

All-purpose flour for dusting

3 large apples, such as Macoun, Empire, or Northern Spy, peeled and shredded

½ cup shredded sharp Cheddar

½ cup dried sweetened cranberries

1 large egg, beaten with a little water

3 tablespoons granulated sugar

1 Line two rimmed baking sheets with nonstick baking liners or parchment paper.

2 Cut the single sheet of puff pastry into two equal and roughly square pieces. Place one piece, covered, in the refrigerator while you work with the other.

3 On a lightly floured surface, roll the pastry out to a 10-by-10-inch square. Using a sharp knife, cut the square into four 5-by-5-inch squares.

4 In the center of each square, place 3 tablespoons of the apple shreds, 1 tablespoon of the cheese shreds, and 1 tablespoon of the dried cranberries. Brush the pastry edges of each with the beaten egg and fold it over, forming a triangle. Crimp each closed with the tines of a fork.

5 Repeat steps 2 through 4 with the remaining refrigerated piece of puff pastry. When all eight pies are formed, carefully transfer them to the prepared baking sheets, leaving 1 inch or so between them.

6 Brush the tops of each with the remaining beaten egg and sprinkle each with 1 generous teaspoon of sugar. Cut two air vents in the top of each. Refrigerate 30 minutes.

7 While the pies are chilling, heat the oven to 375°F.

8 Bake until deeply golden brown, about 25 minutes, switching the baking sheets halfway through. Remove from the oven. Allow to cool for a few minutes before removing to a cooling rack.

9 Serve warm or at room temperature.

CHOCOLATE ZUCCHINI CAKE

Makes 12 servings

Vermont has a zucchini problem. This recipe first caught my eye in an old church cookbook for its unexpected touches of cinnamon and orange. Then I realized that it had been contributed by a friend's mother. "I would often come home to find someone's 'generous' gift of many zucchinis on my doorstep," explained Maggie Trombley. She glazes the cake, but I like it simply dusted with confectioners' sugar.

FOR THE CAKE

Cooking spray for greasing

2½ cups all-purpose flour

½ cup Dutch process cocoa powder

2½ teaspoons baking powder

1½ teaspoons baking soda

1 teaspoon ground cinnamon

½ teaspoon fine salt

2 cups granulated sugar

¾ cup vegetable oil

3 large eggs

2 cups (¾ pound) coarsely shredded zucchini

2 teaspoons pure vanilla extract

2 teaspoons freshly grated orange zest

½ cup milk

1 cup chopped walnuts, optional

FOR THE GLAZE

2 cups confectioners' sugar

3 tablespoons milk

1 teaspoon pure vanilla extract

Make the cake:

1 Heat the oven to 350°F. Generously grease a large (10- to 12-cup) Bundt pan with the cooking spray.

2 In a medium bowl, whisk together the flour, cocoa powder, baking powder, baking soda, cinnamon, and salt.

3 In a stand mixer fitted with the paddle attachment (or using a handheld electric mixer), beat together the sugar and oil. Add the eggs, one at a time, beating well and scraping down the bowl after each addition. Using a spoon, stir in the zucchini, vanilla extract, and orange zest.

4 Add one-third of the flour mixture and ¼ cup of the milk to the sugar mixture. Using the stand or electric mixer, mix just until blended. Add the next one-third of the flour mixture and the remaining ¼ cup milk and mix just until blended. Finish by mixing in the remaining one-third of the flour mixture and the walnuts, if using, until just combined.

5 Pour the batter into the prepared pan. Bake until the top is golden brown and a cake tester comes out clean, about 50 minutes. Remove from the oven.

6 Transfer the cake in the pan to a cooling rack and set aside to cool about 15 minutes.

7 Lay a serving plate larger than the Bundt pan on top of the cake and carefully flip it over. Using a spoon, knock on the outside of the Bundt pan to help release the cake before lifting the pan off the serving plate.

Make the glaze:

1 In a medium bowl, whisk together the confectioners' sugar, milk, and vanilla until smooth.

2 Drizzle the glaze over the cooled cake or just dust the cake with a little confectioners' sugar right before serving.

MAPLE GINGER COOKIES

Makes 20 3-inch cookies

In this Vermont spin on the classic molasses gingersnap, I use dark maple syrup to make these soft and chewy cookies. They're always a crowd-pleaser, but they're a showstopper when used in ice cream sandwiches inspired by the state's most famous food company, Ben & Jerry's.

To make ice cream sandwiches: Buy a pint of ice cream packaged in a cardboard container. Set the pint horizontally on a cutting board and, using your sharpest large knife, cut ½-inch slices crosswise from the pint of ice cream. Snip the ring of cardboard off each slice. Press each round of ice cream between two cookies. Either eat right away or freeze wrapped tightly in foil or plastic wrap. If frozen, soften the sandwiches at room temperature for 5 to 10 minutes before serving.

2 cups all-purpose flour

2 teaspoons baking soda

1 teaspoon ground cinnamon

½ teaspoon ground ginger

½ teaspoon fine salt

8 tablespoons (1 stick) unsalted butter, at room temperature

4 tablespoons (½ stick) vegetable shortening, at room temperature

½ cup light brown sugar, firmly packed

1 cup granulated sugar

1 large egg

¼ cup dark maple syrup

1 Heat the oven to 375°F. Line two rimmed baking sheets with non-stick baking liners or parchment paper.

2 In a medium bowl, whisk together the flour, baking soda, cinnamon, ginger, and salt.

3 Using a stand mixer fitted with the paddle attachment, cream together the butter, shortening, brown sugar, and ½ cup of the granulated sugar until pale and fluffy. Beat in the egg and syrup.

4 In batches, gradually add the flour mixture to the wet mixture, beating just until combined and occasionally scraping down the sides of the bowl.

5 Using a tablespoon measure, scoop out 2 tablespoons of dough and roll into a golf ball–size round. Repeat until all dough has been formed into balls. Roll the balls in the remaining ½ cup sugar until well coated and place on the prepared baking sheets, leaving 2 inches of space between each dough ball.

6 Bake the cookies in batches until they are set around the edges but still soft in the center, about 10 minutes. Remove from the oven and set aside to cool 5 minutes. Transfer to a cooling rack to cool completely.

7 Serve or store.

ACKNOWLEDGMENTS

With deep gratitude to the farmers, cheesemakers, orchardists, foragers and wildcrafters, hunters, sugarmakers, beekeepers, bakers, butchers, brewers, cidermakers, winemakers, distillers, cooks, and chefs who have educated and inspired me over the last 20-plus years. It is thanks to you that I have learned to savor and create delicious food and drink from the fields, waters, and forests of Vermont.

Love to my always supportive family: Mark, who almost always likes what I cook but eats it either way; Nikko and Alex, who grew up as recipe guinea pigs and are now cooking for themselves; Mum, for instilling in me her love of cooking; and Julia, Alexis, Marc, and Carol for wonderful meals cooked and shared together—though not nearly often enough.

For keeping me laughing and dancing through it all, hugs to you, dear friends.

And a final thank-you for bringing this sweet little book project my way: Jessie, for thinking of me; Leslie, for your trust and support throughout; and Katie, for serendipitous connections that go way back.

INDEX

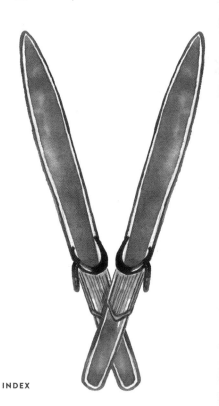